Sexual Sin

Combatting the Drifting and Cheating

Jeffrey S. Black

P U B L I S H I N G

P.O. BOX 817 • PHILLIPSBURG • NEW JERSEY 08865-0817

Printed in the United States of America

Library of Congress Cataloging-in-Publication Data

Black, Jeffrey S., 1954–
    Sexual sin : combatting the drifting and cheating / Jeffrey S. Black.
        p.   cm.—(Resources for changing lives)
      ISBN 0-87552-690-X
    1. Lust—Religious aspects—Christianity. 2. Sex—Religious aspects—Christianity. 3. Adultery. I. Title. II. Series.

BV4627.L8 B58 2003
241'.66—dc21

                           2002192680

Sexual Sin

Combatting the
Drifting and Cheating

Resources for Changing Lives

A Ministry of
THE CHRISTIAN COUNSELING AND
EDUCATIONAL FOUNDATION
Glenside, Pennsylvania

RCL Ministry Booklets
Susan Lutz, Series Editor

I once counseled a man who had been involved in a series of sex crimes. He had been caught, arrested, and indicted by the time his lawyer referred him to me. A believer in his late fifties, he was a widower with several children who lived out of state. At the time the sex crimes were committed, his wife had been dead for about ten years.

The marriage had been very troubled. There had been fights and he'd been thrown out of the house. His wife had been hospitalized on a number of occasions for depression. During those times the couple obviously had no sexual involvement, and the man told me that he had had several affairs while his wife had been unavailable sexually. He seemed to think that made them less objectionable.

This man also told me that he had had several exploratory homosexual relationships, prior to his marriage, in his late teens and early twenties. During his marriage and after his wife's death, he had had a very close relationship with his daughter, so intense that I thought perhaps there had been some incestuous things going on, but he said no. However, it was clear that his daughter had functioned in other ways as a surrogate spouse for him. When she was in her thirties, she decided to move away. Approximately a year after that, he began sexual involvements with two teenage boys.

Sexual Immorality as "Cheating"

This man's story illustrates two ways of thinking about sexual sin. The first is what I call sexual immorality as a way of "cheating." Typically, we think of cheating in terms of having an affair with somebody who is not your spouse. My meaning here is a little different. Ephesians 5:31–32 reads:

> "For this reason a man will leave his father and mother and be united to his wife, and the two will become one flesh." This is a profound mystery—but I am talking about Christ and the church. However, each one of you also must love his wife as he loves himself, and the wife must respect her husband.

Scripture is very clear that God intends marriage to be an expression or a metaphor for our relationship with Christ. It is intended to mirror the profound, mysterious, spiritual union that takes place when we come into our relationship with him. Paul states in Galatians 2 that in some sense we've been *united* with Christ. Christ has become part of us; we've been indwelt by his Spirit. Clearly, it's a mystical and spiritual union for which human vocabulary falls short.

Marriage is intended to picture that relationship as an expression of intense companionship and intimacy. Scripture says that two become one. And God says that sexuality in a marriage relationship is supposed to be an expression of that companionship, an expression and consequence of that intimacy.

In 1 Corinthians 6:15–17, Paul is talking about sexual immorality:

> Do you not know that your bodies are members of Christ himself? Shall I then take the members of Christ and unite them with a prostitute? Never! Do you not know that he who unites himself with a prostitute is one with her in body? For it is said, "The two will become one flesh." But he who unites himself with the Lord is one with him in spirit.

Sexuality is a way of physically identifying and experiencing oneness. In my opinion, sexuality is supposed to be the expression of a oneness *that already exists*. Interestingly, the world reverses that. It says that if you want to experience oneness, you have sex with someone. God says "No." You have oneness first, and your sex has meaning only when it expresses a unity that already exists. Sexual union never *produces* intimacy; it only enhances it. Or perhaps, in some sense, completes it.

Sex Without Intimacy

The desire for sex in a relationship that otherwise lacks intimacy is one of the most common complaints in marriage. A husband comes looking for affection, while his wife complains that he never talks, he doesn't listen, and he spends his "down" time in front of the television. "But he always seems to come alive when we go to bed," she notes. Sometimes she will consent to sex, but then gives in to resentment. If this husband thinks that snuggling in bed will draw his wife close to him, he is making a critical mistake. The sex may impact him positively, but it won't produce the communion that his wife longs for and that God prescribes for marriage. God always says that sexuality is supposed to be an expression of a communion that *already* exists.

I call the behavior of my sex-offender counselee "cheating" because his whole sexual life—his marriage, his extramarital affairs, and even the deviant sexual behavior he exhibited—was his attempt to experience sex without intimacy. He was lazy. He didn't want to strive for intimacy in his relationships. He didn't want to strive for it in his relationship with his wife; hence, the adultery. He found his intimacy in a convenient relationship with his daughter, which God says is no place for him to have it. I believe that is one of the reasons his daughter moved away. This man was a cheater. God had laid out a plan, and he ignored that plan to do things his own way.

As I worked with him, I asked about the possibility of getting remarried. He said, "Well, I just don't want another marriage to turn out like my first one." That's understandable, but what was he really saying? He was saying, "I don't want to work at intimacy. I want the consequences of sexuality, but I don't want to achieve it in the way God designs it." After his daughter left, this man began to attach himself to two kids who lived nearby. They began to serve this cheating purpose in his life.

Any time you see a person engage in illicit sexual behavior, you can be sure that he or she is a cheater. He wants sexual gratification without intimacy. That means that when you're trying to help someone who comes with a problem of pornography, a sexual problem in the marriage relationship, or even an involvement in a bizarre and perverted form of sexuality, at root he doesn't want to experience sexuality in the context for which God designed it. This person must be confronted with God's program, and that program is intimacy.

Self-Centeredness and Sex

When you are trying to help people who have problems with pornography, one thing you have to understand is that pornography has a very simple goal. That goal is masturbation. When someone produces a pornographic movie or magazine (in an industry obviously targeted towards men), the goal is masturbation. But more than that, the goal of the pornography and the masturbation is to create a substitute for intimacy.

Masturbation is sex with yourself. If I'm having sex with myself, I don't have to invest myself in another person. People who are "addicted" to

6

pornography aren't so much addicted to lurid material as they're addicted to self-centeredness. They're committed to serving themselves, to doing whatever they can to find a convenient way not to die to self, which is the nature of companionship in a relationship.

The self-centeredness shows up in many different ways. For example, there are some pedophiles who view even preadolescent children as adult sexual partners. In these instances they don't think, "I want to have sex with a child." Instead, they see the child as their sexual, physical, and emotional equal. To do otherwise would be to de-center, to *not* see everything through the lens of their own experience. That is dying to self, that's intimacy, that's companionship, that's loving somebody else, which is precisely what these individuals are unwilling to do.

Scripture offers the very best model for understanding this kind of sexual sin. The psychological literature offers countless explanations for these behaviors that are all designed *not* to end up focusing on you. They are designed to end up preoccupied with your history, your traumatic experiences, and your mother. They are not designed to end up with you.

But Scripture always focuses on the heart.

Because God plans sexuality to be an expression of oneness, any form of sexual perversion is a perversion of God's plan of intimacy. Whether you are trying to help a person whose sexual behavior makes you physically ill or someone with "garden variety" sexual problems in marriage, the problems always go back to the image of intimacy because that is the root of God's intention for sexuality. Genesis 2:18—"It is not good for the man to be alone"—means that your most basic goal is to teach this person to die to self and to love others more than himself or herself.

Intimacy or Addiction?

While counseling the man I described earlier, I received a phone call from his attorney. The attorney was a believer and sympathetic to biblical counseling, but he wanted his client to attend a sex addicts clinic in the belief that the judge would then give him a lighter sentence. I believed that the man was no longer a threat. He seemed well grounded at that point and I did not want to see him go to jail. I believed he had repented and that he was doing some good work in counseling. So I agreed.

What a mistake! He didn't go to jail, but in

order to get a favorable sentence, he had to label himself as a sex addict and withdraw from other relationships until he was "cured." As a consequence, my prescription for this man backfired. I wanted him to pursue legitimate intimacy in the context of marriage for the first time in his life. But because of the sex addict label, he was isolated from everyone—except other sex addicts. The court's goal was to keep him out of any meaningful relationship—the very root of the problem. My new challenge was to figure out how to implement the things I knew he needed when everything I wanted him to do is what the court *didn't* want him to do.

Sexual Immorality as "Drifting"

The second aspect of sexual immorality is "drift," which is what I call a history of the heart. Let me give you an illustration.

When I was seventeen, I decided to buy my first pornographic magazine. This was a fearsome thing to me. I remember going to the local drugstore that had a little magazine section. I waited and watched to make sure nobody was looking. I picked up the magazine and rolled it up so you couldn't see what it was. Then I stood around and wandered back and forth until I screwed up the courage to pay for it. Just as I walked towards the counter, the man behind the counter left and a woman took his place. I quickly turned around. I must have spent forty-five minutes in that store trying to buy that magazine—but I did manage to buy it. As time passed, I bought a few more.

Then I noticed something. I wasn't rolling up the magazine any more. I just picked it up, walked to the counter, and bought it! As a matter of fact, I started buying two. I still bought them only when the man was there. But after a while, I didn't care who was behind the counter. Eventually I was even able to chat with the woman when I paid for the magazines.

A Shifting Comfort Zone

People start out in what I call a baseline comfort zone in the way they deal with their own sin. God says that the nature of sin is such that as we continue to sin, as we continue to quench the Spirit, as we continue to sear our consciences, what was originally a very un-comfortable thing to do becomes comfortable. We begin to drift as we compromise. We started at one point and it was a terrible, anxi-ety-provoking experience. But because of our lust, our desire, our heart set against God, after a while this reaction fades. We are in a new comfort zone. And after awhile, if we do not repent, we drift even further.

As we do, we simultaneously move further and further away from God. Interestingly, the Scriptures describe the impact of our sin on the Holy Spirit in emotionally intimate terms. It is not just human beings who are hurt by our sin! Believers are reminded and warned not to insult the Spirit (Heb. 10:28–29); not to quench the Spirit (1 Thess. 5:19–22); and not to provoke or grieve the Spirit (Eph. 4:29–32). Clearly, God takes our sin personally. The images of grieving and quenching the Holy Spirit suggest that a repetitive pattern of sin, in this case sexual sin, will separate, distance, or at least influence the Spirit's ministry to the individual. At least subjectively, if not in fact, the comeback from bondage is tougher and sometimes more traumatic; the damage is greater; and the kind of faith necessary to move out of the pit seems more difficult to come by. The lesson of the Prodigal Son teaches us that God is thrilled to receive us back as our hearts turn toward him (Luke 15:20). But how much better it is not to go away at all!

Any time you minister to somebody with a

sexual problem, especially somebody with what we'd consider a severe or deviant sexual problem, that person has a history of sin in that area. Nobody gets up in the morning and says, "I don't have anything to do today. I think I'll go expose myself! I was headed to the mall anyway." We never leap into extreme forms of sin. We always *drift* into them. Thus, you should assume that the person has a lengthy history of immorality that he will be reluctant to reveal to you.

Typically, when you ask such persons what they did, they will tell you. But when you ask, "What else did you do? What led up to that?," they will answer, "I didn't do anything else." You wait. "What else did you do?" "I didn't do anything. That's it." Don't believe them. Keep asking. This is the nature of the sinful, human heart. Invariably as you spend time with the person, you begin to see a history of compromise in his life that makes the last thing not a leap but a baby step. In terms of sexual sin, he had already drifted far away from God's standards.

Sinful "drift" is like going to the beach and falling asleep on a raft. All of a sudden your sleep is disturbed by the lifeguard's whistle. You ask yourself, *What idiot is he whistling at?* You look up, and it's you! You hadn't planned it, but suddenly every body on the beach looks like a little dot because you've drifted way out to sea. That's the way sin works. Sin always has a history. But remember that God also has a history with our hearts.

God's History with Our Hearts

That history is called our sanctification, the process by which believers' hearts and lives become more and more like Christ's (Eph. 4:22–24). Sanctification is both positionally complete and dynamically progressive. It is complete because the process is based on Christ's finished work on the cross, which removes our sins and gives us the righteousness of Christ (2 Cor. 5:21). It is dynamically progressive because our new status in Christ becomes a daily reality as we follow Christ by faith and allow the Holy Spirit to change our hearts (Titus 2:11–14).

As the following Scripture passages make clear, the Spirit uses the Word of God in that process. Psalm 119:9–11 reads, "How can a young man keep his way pure? By living according to your word. I seek you with all my heart; do not let me stray from your commands. I have hidden your word in my heart that I might not sin against you." In John 17:14–19 Jesus prays to the Father,

> "I have given them your word and the world has hated them, for they are not of the world any more than I am of the world. My prayer is not that you would take them out of the world but that you protect them from the evil one. They are not of the world, even as I am not of it. Sanctify them by the truth; your word is truth. As you sent me into the world, I have sent them into the world. For them I sanctify myself, that they too may be truly sanctified."

The person who drifts lives in a heart world of compromise and immorality. He is continually thinking his own thoughts and scheming his schemes. But the believer is called to sanctify himself by meditating on the Word of God. The book of James tells us that there is an important distinction between the temptation that may lead the heart into sexual sin (James 1:14) and the sin itself. Men and women who battle with sexual sin are wise to strengthen their hearts against the power of a specific temptation. How? By a general, baseline obedience to the Word of God. This obedience rests on a deep confidence that Christ's death has not only delivered them from the sin that tempts them, but will also give them the strength to put it to death in their lives (Rom. 8:11–14). This is God's solution to the sexual sins that trouble and torment many.

This is why the Bible doesn't have anything specific to say about masturbation. It doesn't need to. The problem with masturbation isn't masturbation but the condition of a person's heart. Masturbation is merely one expression of that condition. Scripture is not inadequate, as some would say, because it doesn't spell out a step-by-step formula for dealing with it. God says that if my heart is kept pure by continually meditating on the Word in the context of God's sanctifying work, I will have the power to overcome the temptations that lead to indulgence, pornography, and masturbation.

Problem-Centered or Heart-Centered?

Most people seek help in counseling because they are problem-centered. They're asking for a technique to prevent them from engaging in a certain behavior. They are hoping for a crash course to help them utilize God to overcome a particular sin. Their desire for a quick solution may be understandable, but there is no technique, no mechanism—psychological, spiritual, or otherwise—that will prevent you from indulging in pornography or masturbation. What we need is God's sanctifying Word continually at work in our lives.

But when God's sanctifying Word has not been steadily at work in people, they will discover in a crisis that they're not equipped to deal with their sin. They hope to find a solution that bypasses that ongoing work of the Spirit through the Word. In essence they say, "Quick! I need a little bit of God! I'm really in trouble here."

As a friend, discipler, or counselor, you can't give people something that God slowly perfects day by day. However, you can offer them biblical guidance, your prayers, and your support as a member of the body of Christ—all of which they need, and all of which will be helpful. What they really need is the wisdom of Christ that changes their hearts, which comes when God applies his Word to their lives and they respond in faith and obedience. In the midst of a crisis, you can encourage the beginning of that process.

"Set Apart" for God or the World

As we deal with the problem of sexual sin, it is important to acknowledge another factor at work. What the Bible calls "the world" is a system of values and beliefs that aggressively seeks control of your heart. The world also has (if I can use this expression) a "sanctifying" influence, in the sense that the world seeks to set us apart for *it*self in contrast to God's desire to set us apart for *him*self. A person who comes seeking help for sexual sins is a person who has been "set apart" by the world, who has allowed himself to continually indulge in the things presented to him by the world.

We must return to the biblical fact that sexuality is a spiritual act; it's not primarily physical. It always involves the person's spirit, either in accord with the will of God, communing with the Holy Spirit, or in rebellion against that will, trying to push the Holy Spirit out of the way.

In contrast, the world presents sexuality as a biological act in what I call a hydraulic model of pressure. We often hear about people having "sexual tension." We are told that their sexual tension will build up and that when they have sex, their sexual tension is released.

After a while it builds up until it is again released. When the pressure is building, the world implies that we are powerless to resist. Sometimes, even Christians think that way and misquote 1 Corinthians 7:1–8 to bolster their argument that marriage is a provision for passion: "Paul says it's better to marry than to burn."

But as many married men have discovered, the flesh is insatiable. It does not operate on the principle of tension release. The human heart is insatiably pursuing evil. As Jeremiah 17:9 summarizes, "The heart is deceitful above all things and beyond cure." That is the problem sexual sin reveals and God's Word addresses. We need to have our hearts continually sanctified before God.

In that sense, everywhere I look in Scripture I see the issue of *porneia* addressed, the issues of masturbation, pornography, sexual perversion, child molestation, pedophilia, and all the other things people get into. The Bible does have a lot to say about them, but not from a technique standpoint; the issue is not psychological techniques. The issue is that God intended sexuality to be an expression of communion and intimacy. It's a metaphor for our relationship with Christ. We seem to find all manner of ways to avoid that reality.

Sexuality is primarily a spiritual act, not a biological one. It's not a problem of dealing with our drives but of sanctifying our hearts. When you seek to help people, you want to keep that in the forefront of their minds. Often, when people come for help, they are terribly disappointed with a biblical approach because they want a solution that doesn't require them to subject their wills to the Holy Spirit. Simply put, their approach to the problem *is* the problem.

But Christians who have committed themselves by faith to obey God's Word are strengthening themselves spiritually through that obedience. Like well-conditioned athletes, they will be better equipped and empowered to resist the specific enemy or desire, because they have submitted their hearts to the work of the Spirit. As they allow him to complete Christ's redemptive work in their lives, they can affirm what the psalmist says: if I hide God's Word in my heart, I will not sin against him.

Jeffrey S. Black is associate pastor at Calvary Chapel in Philadelphia and an adjunct faculty member of the Christian Counseling and Educational Foundation's School of Biblical Counseling in Glenside, Pennsylvania.

RCL Ministry Booklets